SO-ARK-647

FAMOUS IMMIGRANT
SCIENTISTS

MAKING AMERICA GREAT
IMMIGRANT SUCCESS STORIES

FAMOUS IMMIGRANT
SCIENTISTS

Enslow Publishing
101 W. 23rd Street
Suite 240
New York, NY 10011
USA
enslow.com

Published in 2018 by Enslow Publishing, LLC.
101 W. 23rd Street, Suite 240, New York, NY 10011

Library of Congress Cataloging-in-Publication Data

Names: Lo Bosco, Maryellen, author.
Title: Famous immigrant scientists / by Maryellen Lo Bosco.
Description: New York : Enslow, 2018. | Series: Making America great: immigrant success stories | Includes bibliographical references and index. | Audience: Grades 7 to 12.
Identifiers: LCCN 2017015082 | ISBN 9780766092440 (library bound) | ISBN 9780766095908 (paperback)
Subjects: LCSH: Scientists—United States—Biography—Juvenile literature. | Immigrants—United States—Biography—Juvenile literature. | Science—United States—History—Juvenile literature.
Classification: LCC Q141 .L75 2018 | DDC 509.22—dc23
LC record available at https://lccn.loc.gov/2017015082

Printed in the United States of America

To Our Readers: We have done our best to make sure all websites in this book were active and appropriate when we went to press. However, the author and the publisher have no control over and assume no liability for the material available on those websites or on any websites they may link to. Any comments or suggestions can be sent by email to customerservice@enslow.com.

Photo credits: Cover, pp. 3, 78–79, 83 NASA/Getty Images; pp. 6–7 Guillaume Plisson/Bloomberg/ Getty Images; pp. 10–11 William Henry Jackson/Hulton Archive/Getty Images; pp. 13, 28, 30 Library of Congress Prints and Photographs Division; pp. 14–15, 50, 76–77 Bettmann/Getty Images; pp. 18–19, 66–67, 97 © AP Images; pp. 24, 32–33 Science & Society Picture Library/Getty Images; p. 26 Aleksandra Pikalova/Shutterstock.com; p. 36 Print Collector/Hulton Archive/Getty Images; pp. 38–39 NYPL/Science Source/Getty Images; p. 41 Library of Congress/Science Faction/Getty Images; pp. 43, 47, 88–89 Corbis Historical/Getty Images; pp. 54–55 Vincent Isore/IP3/Getty Images; pp. 56–57 Vitaly Nevar/TASS/Getty Images; p. 60 Tim Mosenfelder/Getty Images; pp. 62–63 Los Alamos National Laboratory/The LIFE Images Collection/Getty Images; pp. 68–69 igorstevanovic/Shutterstock.com; p. 73 Robert Sullivan/AFP/Getty Images; p. 81 Rex Features/AP Images; p. 87 Prisma/Universal Images Group/Getty Images; pp. 92–93 Lloyd Fox/Baltimore Sun/Tribune News Service /Getty Images; cover and interior pages Saicle/Shutterstock.com (flag).

Contents

Introduction

Any number of things can make a country great: abundant natural resources, a mild climate, a variety of growing seasons, and mountains, beaches, and oceans, to name a few. A great country has stunning natural beauty, a variety of wildlife, and many plants. A truly fortunate country is home to many different people from every corner of the globe. Behind every great country is a great people. In the United States, many of those people have come from somewhere else.

To be on the cutting edge, a nation needs the best scientists. Many of America's scientists have been and continue to be immigrants. Since the beginning of its history, America's immigrant scientists have played important roles in making the United States a world leader. Science and technology are responsible for the growth of cities and help people to live longer and have a better quality of life. Science is our best hope for solving the problems of a world with a growing population of close to 7.5 billion people.

The world will turn to science and technology in the coming years to solve the problems of climate change and the destruction of nature. Science will be necessary to help stop food and water shortages and improve health and medical care. Scientists will have the job of curbing the use of weapons of mass destruction. Researchers in the United States are hard at work on today's problems, but many immigrant scientists ran into barriers in their home countries. Once they arrived in the United States, they made powerful contributions to the country and the world.

It takes twelve years for a new medicine to get from the laboratory to consumers' medicine cabinets. The scientists who make these drugs include immigrants on H-1B visas, which allow noncitizens with special skills to work for American companies.

For example, Joseph Priestley discovered oxygen, and Nikola Tesla helped make electricity available to the masses. Albert Einstein rocked the world of physics with his special and general theories of relativity. The atomic bomb would not have been built without Enrico Fermi, and Elias Zerhouni developed new MRI imaging techniques. Also, Gerti Theresa Cori's work with sugar metabolism has shed more light on diabetes.

Elizabeth Blackburn spotted the secrets of telomeres, the protective caps on the ends of chromosomes that reveal the state of cell health. Gebisa Ejeta created sorghum hybrid plants that greatly increased crop yield—a crucial development in countries where sorghum is a big part of the diet. Kaplana Chawla and Franklin Chang-Díaz traveled beyond Earth on the space shuttle to learn more about the solar system, and Chang-Díaz is working on a rocket propulsion system that will take us to Mars and back.

Only by keeping its doors open can the United States continue to benefit from immigrant talent. Immigrants arrive on these shores in search of the American dream. They hope for more freedom, independence, and a chance to fulfill their dreams. Successful immigrants help to make their adopted country great.

CHAPTER 1

WHOSE LAND IS IT ANYWAY? A SHORT HISTORY OF US IMMIGRATION

This land is your land, this land is my land
From California to the New York Island
From the Redwood Forest, to the Gulf stream waters
This land was made for you and me.
   —From "This Land Is Your Land" by Woody Guthrie[1]

"This Land is Your Land," written by activist, singer, and guitar player Woody Guthrie, is perhaps the most well-known American folk song. Guthrie wrote the song in 1940 at the end of the Great Depression. After traveling the country and seeing the misery of the poor, the musician wrote his song as an anthem of unity. He thought the land should belong to all the people—not just the people who could buy it. In 1940, the descendants of Europeans owned the majority of land "from sea to shining sea." They had taken almost all of the land from Native Americans who had lived on it for thousands of years before the Europeans arrived.

As early as 1783, the new American nation was a diverse society. It included hundreds of Native American tribes, European settlers, and West Africans—brought as slaves to the United States and forced to work, often on large pieces of land known as plantations. Less than a century later, the country would fight the American Civil War, which led to the freedom of some four million black men, women, and children living without any human rights. In 1868, the Fourteenth Amendment to the Constitution was ratified, granting citizenship to black Americans. Even though they'd lived on the land longer than anyone, Native Americans did not receive US citizenship until 1924.

As time went on and newer technology made it easier to cross the Atlantic Ocean, increasing numbers of Europeans arrived in the United States seeking opportunities that had run out or weren't available back home. This land became the "melting pot" of all nations. Americans often hear that the United States has welcomed people of all ethnic groups and religions, but history shows that this is not true—the United States has not always been kind to minority groups and immigrants. At the same time, there is no denying that immigrants have helped the United States excel in the sciences and other fields.

Both the Plains Indians, such as the Pawnees, and the tribes east of the Mississippi River were forced to settle in Oklahoma Territory after the passage of the Indian Removal Act of 1830.

Still, the United States continues to face questions about which people have a right to live here and which do not. The chapters that follow will look at some of the immigrants who helped make America great. But before we turn to them, let's briefly review the history of immigration in America.

THE COLONIAL PERIOD

After Christopher Columbus landed in the Caribbean in 1492, the Spanish settled throughout the Americas. Great Britain began its first successful colony in Jamestown, Virginia, in 1607, followed by another settlement in Plymouth, Massachusetts, in 1620. By the end of the sixteenth century, the Spanish had settled in Florida. In the seventeenth century, the British established thirteen colonies on the East Coast, although the settlers came from a variety of countries. Europeans brought enslaved Africans to the colonies as early as 1619. When the American Revolution began in 1775, 2.5 million Europeans and Africans already lived in the colonies.

From the time it was founded, the United States has served as a haven for those seeking civil, religious, and economic freedom. The first census of the American republic, taken in 1790, counted 3.9 million people. Almost 20 percent of these individuals came from Africa. Little immigration happened in the first decade of the 1800s, but following the War of 1812 (between the British and the Americans), immigration from Western Europe increased.

THE NINETEENTH CENTURY

From 1820 to 1880, immigrants came from northern and central Europe, Canada, and China, and enslaved people were brought from Africa. The Chinese began arriving on the West Coast in the 1850s, drawn by the California gold rush. They helped build the

Christopher Columbus's actual name was Cristoforo Colombo, and though he sailed under the Spanish flag, he was a native of Italy. He never set foot on the North American continent, landing in the Bahamas on his first voyage in 1492.

transcontinental railroad from 1863 to 1869.

During the Civil War of the 1860s, many Americans supported immigration. But the Know-Nothing Party, also called the American Party, opposed immigration. In 1862, the Homestead Act passed, which encouraged immigrants to move to the western territories. Citizens and immigrants could buy land at $1.25 per acre, and many people took advantage of the US Congress's sale of public lands. By the 1880s, immigrants came from the Middle East, the Mediterranean, and southern and eastern Europe.

THE TWENTIETH CENTURY

As time passed and the country grew and became more diverse, immigration policy became less friendly. Congress passed the Chinese Exclusion Act in 1882, which severely limited Chinese immigration between 1882 and 1904. Additionally, the 1917 Immigration Act barred immigration from most of Southeast Asia

The California gold rush brought fortune hunters from many countries, including China. When the gold ran out, the Chinese became a target of discrimination, which reached its peak in 1882 with the Chinese Exclusion Act—halting Chinese immigration.

and almost all of the Middle East. The United States also halted immigration from Japan. But the government continued to welcome immigrants from Mexico and Europe, including Russian Jews and Armenians fleeing persecution.

In 1921, the Emergency Quota Act began limiting immigrants by nationality. The government used the 1910 census to determine the number of immigrants to let in from certain countries. No more than 3 percent of any one ethnic group could enter the United States. With this formula, more northern Europeans entered the country than people from any other region.

The 1924 National Origins Act was more extreme than the Emergency Quota Act. No more than 2 percent of people from any ethnic group could come to the United States. And instead of using the 1910 census as a guide, the government used the 1890 census. But immigrants continued to enter the country between 1880 and 1930, with about twenty-eight million people total coming to the United States, many from southern and eastern Europe.

THE EUGENICS MOVEMENT AND IMMIGRATION

At the peak of immigration, about 15 percent of the American population was foreign born. In large cities, immigrants made up more than 50 percent of the population. The new immigrants were darker, not Protestant, and did not speak English. White Americans with roots in western Europe viewed them as more "foreign" than immigrants from Great Britain, Germany, and Scandinavia. They considered them less educated, less skilled, and less intelligent than previous immigrants.

Fear of foreigners led to more interest in eugenics, the so-called science of improving "human stock" through breeding.

FRANZ BOAS AND CULTURAL RELATIVITY

Franz Boas, a German Jewish immigrant with a PhD in physics and geography, spoke out against the racism of people like Charles Davenport and Harry Laughlin. Boas became the first professor of anthropology at Columbia University. He researched the Eskimos in the Arctic Circle and questioned the idea that one culture was superior to another. Instead, he said that this idea was a matter of opinion. By doing so, he challenged the idea that Western civilization was better than others.

He was the first major Western scholar to state that people of all ethnicities were equal. Boas's book, *The Mind of Primitive Man*, a series of lectures on culture and race, was used to oppose those who supported immigration limits for people deemed racially inferior. In the 1930s, Germany revoked Boas's PhD, and the Nazis burned copies of his book. In the 1930s and 1940s, he lectured widely and wrote on the subject of race, warning people about the dangers of Nazism.

In 1910, Charles Davenport, a Harvard-educated zoologist who taught biology at both Harvard University and the University of Chicago, founded the Eugenics Record Office in Cold Spring Harbor, New York, using money from the Carnegie Foundation to start the program. His organization collected family records of people viewed as "unfit" to breed.

In 1969, the Center for Disease Control deliberately continued the infamous Tuskegee Study, begun in 1932, which withheld treatment for syphilis from a group of black men. Only after the press exposed the study was it discontinued in 1972.

Harry Laughlin served as superintendent of the organization. He had a PhD from Princeton University in the field of cytology (the study of cells). Laughlin had major influence on immigration policy in the United States. He gave testimony to Congress in support of the Immigration Act of 1924. He claimed that immigrants from Southern and Eastern Europe had higher levels of insanity, and he drafted a "model law" to force such immigrants to be sterilized, which would stop them from having children. The Nazis used Laughlin's model for their own sterilization law in 1933.

In fact, the government forced about sixty thousand Americans to get sterilized. As late as the 1970s, some mental patients continued to be sterilized against their will. The eugenics movement was not the only example of bad science. Researchers used groups without full civil rights, such as blacks, women, the mentally ill, prisoners, immigrants, and the disabled, for medical experiments. Often scientists conducted the experiments without telling their test subjects. One well-known example of medical experimentation took place in the twentieth century, when black men with syphilis were studied and left untreated for forty years as part of the Tuskegee Study.

THE INTERNMENT OF THE ETHNIC JAPANESE

When the United States entered World War II in 1941, the government rounded up Japanese Americans and Japanese immigrants and sent them to internment camps. US citizens made up more than 60 percent of this group, who were forced to live in the camps until the end of the war.

The government said Japanese Americans and Japanese immigrants posed a national security threat. Officials believed that they might spy on the country for Japan, but historians now say racism played a bigger role in the decision. The government used the Alien Enemies Act to place the ethnic Japanese into camps, and this act remains law today.

The ethnic Japanese lost most of their wealth, since the government took their homes and farms away. While the government also detained German and Italian immigrants living in the United States, it did not round them up in large numbers or intern US citizens of Italian or German heritage. The government forced about 120,000 ethnic Japanese into camps. No Japanese American or Japanese immigrant tried to betray the US government.

CHANGES TO IMMIGRATION LAW

The Immigration and Nationality Act of 1952 changed many previous immigration laws, though it retained a national-origin quota system. Later, the Immigration and Nationality Act of 1965 ended the quota system. In 1968, the government outlawed exclusion of immigrants based on race, sex, or nationality. It also added new immigration criteria—such as family ties, refugee status, and skill sets. As a result of these changes, Asian immigration increased, particularly from India, and the United States gained access to a wide pool of engineering and science talent.

The Refugee Act of 1980 started a process for admitting both refugees and asylum seekers. The Immigration and Reform and Control Act of 1986 made it harder for employers to hire undocumented immigrants, but it also created two programs that led many people living in the United States without papers since 1982 to become "legal." The law also gave some farmworkers the chance to become permanent residents. Under this program, close to three million people became permanent residents. Today, some eleven million undocumented immigrants live in the United States, but lawmakers have not agreed on a way to put them on the path to citizenship.

IMMIGRATION IN THE AGE OF TERRORISM

After the 1993 attack on the World Trade Center in New York, the United States passed laws that made it easier to deport and jail immigrants who had committed certain crimes. It also added other ways to monitor and control immigration. The "War on Terror," which began after the September 11, 2001, attacks, continues to affect immigration policy. The 2001 USA PATRIOT Act expanded the reasons the government could use to ban immigrants with possible terrorist ties from entering the United States. Changes to the law also meant the government could keep a closer eye on foreign students. The Homeland Security Act created the Department of Homeland Security in 2002. The department now oversees all functions of the US Citizenship and Immigration Services, US Immigration and Customs Enforcement, and US Customs and Border Protection agencies.

Americans continue to debate immigration. Many would like to see all undocumented immigrants deported, all refugees kept out, and a ban of all people from Muslim-majority countries from entering the United States. It's uncertain how America will balance its need to secure its borders with a humane immigration policy. To ensure that it remains a science and technology leader, it's important that the United States makes room for the talented immigrants who seek to move to the United States from around the world.

CHAPTER 2

EARLY IMMIGRANT SCIENTISTS IN CHEMISTRY AND ELECTRICITY

Joseph Priestley arrived in the United States as a refugee fleeing religious and political persecution. Nikola Tesla came to the country in hopes of finding people to put his ideas to use. Both left their mark on the science world.

JOSEPH PRIESTLEY

Joseph Priestley, born on March 13, 1733, is best known for discovering oxygen, but he also published numerous works on science, theology, politics, education, and history. Priestley disagreed with the ideas of the Church of England, so both the church and the English government treated him badly. His support of the Unitarian religious view, along with the American and French Revolutions, led his countrymen to drive him from his home. He left England in 1794 and settled in Pennsylvania. He became an important voice in the Unitarian movement in the United States.

Priestley was born in the Yorkshire region of northern England. His mother died giving birth

Joseph Priestley is best known for the discovery of oxygen, but he published in many fields besides science, including theology, political philosophy, education, and history. Priestley was forced to emigrate from England because of his dissenting religious views.

to her sixth child, and Joseph was sent away. From the age of nine, he grew up in the house of his father's sister, Sarah Keighley. When Joseph attended school as a young child, he learned Latin, Greek, and Hebrew. As a sickly teen, he taught himself French, Italian, and High Dutch as well as algebra and philosophy. He entered Daventry Academy in 1752 and graduated in 1755. He held many jobs as a minister and teacher.

While studying at the Warrington Academy, he turned his interest to scientific experiments. He started with electricity before taking up chemistry. He met Benjamin Franklin and became a member of the Royal Society of England, the nation's top scientific organization.

THE DISCOVERY OF OXYGEN

Priestley investigated the "airs" using an inverted glass container that could collect the gases below, created by his experiments. He could also put his container into a pool of mercury or water to seal it. He experimented with both fire and mice.

He noticed that when he sealed one of his containers, a mouse would die. But when he put a green plant in the container and exposed it to sunlight, the mouse lived longer. This is because the plant generated oxygen through photosynthesis (the process by which plants use sunlight to create chemical energy), allowing the mouse to breathe. He set apart the oxygen using a twelve-inch-(thirty-centimeter) wide glass with a lump of mercuric oxide and heated the substance with sunlight. Inside the glass, fire burned longer and the mouse lived longer. He also swallowed the oxygen, finding it pleasant.[1]

PRIESTLEY'S WORK IN CHEMISTRY

Priestley moved to Mill Hill Chapel in Leeds in 1767. There, he discovered carbon dioxide and made the first soda water. He received the Copley Medal of Achievement from the Royal Society in 1772, and then continued his investigations, discovering oxygen and several other gases. Priestley called his most important find "dephlogisticated

About fifteen years after Joseph Priestley discovered carbon dioxide, J. J. Schweppe developed a process for making carbonated mineral water and created the Schweppes Company in Geneva in 1783.

air" because he believed it contained a substance called "phlogiston" that was released when something burned. Building on this idea, he determined that oxygen contained no phlogiston and soaked up what was in flammable, or burnable, materials such as wood. Flammable materials burned easily in the presence of this air.

A Swedish chemist, Carl Wilhelm Scheele, isolated the same gas, calling it "fire air," but he didn't publish his findings until 1777. Priestley met the French chemist Antoine-Laurent Lavoisier in 1774 and shared his findings with him, which helped the Frenchman develop his theories on chemical reaction. Lavoisier named the new element oxygen and proved the phlogiston theory wasn't true.

BIRMINGHAM RIOTS

In 1780, Priestley took a job as a senior minister of the New Meeting in Birmingham. He taught, preached, and started many Sunday schools. He also joined a science club called the Lunar Society. But the Church of England disapproved of his religious writings. Priestley didn't believe that Jesus was one of the three entities in the Trinity. The church said Father (God), Son (Jesus), and the Holy Spirit made up the Trinity. But Priestly thought Jesus was totally human, with God-given powers.

He also supported civil and religious freedom and changes to England's lawmaking body—Parliament. He backed the French Revolution as well. European royalty viewed the revolution as a major threat. The English royal family still had a lot of political power, and many people feared the revolution would cause political changes in Great Britain. In July 1791, a "Church and King" mob burned Priestley's home and church to the ground, and he and his family fled to London.

The mob had also destroyed the property of other Birmingham dissenters, and the Priestleys could not return home. Many people

John Adams, second president of the United States, was a political philosopher and early supporter of the American Revolution. He helped negotiate the Treaty of Paris with Great Britain, which ended the war in 1783.

shunned him because of his political and religious views. His sons had already left for America by the time he and his wife moved to the United States in April 1794. They settled in Northumberland, Pennsylvania, even though the University of Pennsylvania in Philadelphia offered Priestly the chance to serve as chemistry chair.

Priestly became friends with both Thomas Jefferson and John Adams. He met Jefferson in 1797, when he traveled to hear him preach in Philadelphia. Three years later, they began writing to each other. In his final days, Priestley continued his scientific work, isolating carbon monoxide, and becoming a voice for English Unitarianism in the United States. This version of Unitarianism had a long influence on the American movement as well as today's Unitarian Universalist churches throughout the United States. Priestly died on February 6, 1804.

NIKOLA TESLA

Nikola Tesla came to America to get the attention of Thomas Edison, thought to be the greatest electrical engineer in the world. He hoped Edison would take an interest in his idea for a motor that ran on AC (alternating current) rather than DC (direct current) electricity.

Tesla was a Serbian American inventor, physicist, and mechanical and electrical engineer. He spoke several languages, had a photographic memory, and slept only a few hours a day, according to many accounts. He won more than 300 patents in his lifetime for different inventions but is best known for designing electrical systems that used AC rather than DC current. AC electricity continues to be used today to power homes and businesses around the world, though the voltage and frequency of the current may vary.

Tesla also created a rotating magnetic field that would allow an AC motor to function. He invented the Tesla coil and the radio, and he was the first to use wireless electricity.

Serbian American inventor Nikola Tesla envisioned some technology he didn't actually complete, such as a system for collecting, encoding, and broadcasting information through a hand-held device.

Tesla was born in 1856 in a small village on the Balkan Peninsula, in a country now called Croatia. His father was an Orthodox Christian priest, while his mother, a homemaker, made her own equipment for the home and farm. She also had a photographic memory. Nikola's father wanted his son to follow him into the priesthood but changed his mind after Nikola became very sick with cholera as a teenager. His father agreed to send him to engineering school if he got better. When young Nikola's health improved, his father let him attend the Polytechnic Institute in Graz, Austria.

AC VERSUS DC

Direct current (DC) flows in one direction, while alternating current (AC) regularly changes directions. Voltage (the amount of power or electricity flowing through a wire) could be easily increased or decreased with a transformer using AC, while DC in Edison's time could not be easily converted to higher or lower voltages.

This meant that DC power plants had to transmit electricity at the same voltage that would be used when the power reached its destination. So, the DC system needed power stations to be located within 1 mile (1.61 km) of the customer, which made it impossible to supply electricity to rural areas and even created problems in big cities.

On the other hand, electricity at high voltages could travel quickly over AC wires and then easily slow down when it reached its destination. This made the use of AC transmission cheaper and more energy efficient than DC transmission.

Tesla was a great student at first, but he became obsessed with his own ideas about a motor that would use alternating current. He stopped paying as much attention to his studies and also took up the bad habit of gambling. As a result, he lost all his tuition money and suffered a nervous breakdown. By 1881, he had recovered and moved to Budapest (Hungary) with a vision of the motor that would use rotating magnetic fields. Then, electric power companies in Austria and France hired him to improve their DC-generation facilities. But Tesla was unable to get anyone interested in his motor.

He arrived in New York in 1884, hoping that Americans would be more open to his ideas than the Europeans. As it turned out, Edison wasn't interested in AC power, since he saw it as competition. Edison's invention of the incandescent, or glowing, lamp had created strong demand for electricity. He had cornered the market using DC power, and he believed it was safer than AC current since it used lower voltages. Tesla briefly worked for Edison, making improvements at Edison's DC generator plants. But he supposedly quit when Edison did not give him the bonus he'd promised.

After Tesla left Edison, he developed a system of AC generators, motors, and transformers, which he sold to George Westinghouse. Tesla's AC induction motor is still widely used in industry and household appliances. Edison was not about to go quietly, however. He competed with Westinghouse by scaring the public about AC power. For example, he publicly electrocuted

Incandescent electric lamps made by Joseph Swan (*left*) and Thomas Edison (*right*) were obsolete by the time the pair joined forces to create the first electric light company. Today's incandescent bulbs are being replaced by more energy-efficient LED lighting.

animals with AC power to prove it was unsafe. But the public got to see AC current in use when Westinghouse won a chance to light up the Chicago World's Fair in 1893. Westinghouse, Tesla, and the large AC generators located in the Fair's Hall of Machinery lit 100,000 incandescent bulbs to create a "City of Light." This marked a turning point for AC and a win for Tesla and Westinghouse.

Two years earlier, in 1891, Tesla became a US citizen. He invented the Tesla coil, a transformer that could produce very high voltages. The coil improved scientists' understanding of electricity. The device also showed that electricity could be generated wirelessly. When Westinghouse won the contract to generate hydroelectric power using Niagara Falls, he used Tesla's designs to build the AC generators. The first illumination from the Falls reached Buffalo at the end of 1896. In a few years, Niagara lit up New York City.

Tesla also developed early neon and fluorescent lighting and was the first to take an X-ray photograph. Tesla would have beaten Marconi in demonstrating wireless telegraphy if his lab hadn't burned down in 1895. However, when Marconi set up long-distance demonstrations of his wireless radio, he used a Tesla oscillator.

Tesla continued to experiment with wireless electricity, but some of his later experiments were too strange for his former backers. His patents had once made him rich, but Tesla died poor on January 7, 1943, in the New Yorker Hotel. A state funeral for the great scientist took place at St. John the Divine Cathedral in New York City with more than 2,000 people in attendance.

CHAPTER 3

IMMIGRANTS WHO USHERED IN THE ATOMIC AGE

A number of refugees came to the United States as a result of the Holocaust. Because so many refugee scientists arrived in the 1930s and early 1940s, the United States became the first nation to build a nuclear weapon.

ALBERT EINSTEIN

German-born Albert Einstein is among the most famous American immigrants. Einstein's theories changed the field of physics and our understanding of the physical world and the universe. Early in his scientific career, Einstein figured out that $E = mc2$ (energy = mass multiplied by the speed of light squared). This discovery paved the way for scientists to transform, through nuclear fission, the mass in uranium into the energy released in the atomic bomb. Nuclear fission involves splitting atoms in a controlled chain reaction. Many countries also use it to generate electricity.

LIFE IN GERMANY

Born in Ulm, Germany, on March 14, 1879, Einstein was the first child of Hermann Einstein and

German-born Albert Einstein revolutionized physics, and his work made possible the building of the first atomic bomb. Worried humanity might destroy itself with its new weapons, Einstein promoted the idea of a world government toward the end of his life.

Pauline Koch Einstein. His parents were ethnic Jews but were not religious. The family moved to Munich when Einstein was a baby. His sister Maja was born a few years later, and they remained close throughout their lives.

His parents did not realize how gifted he was at first. In fact, they worried that he might be developmentally disabled because he was slow to speak. Albert was a disobedient child and often had temper tantrums. He struggled in school from an early age because he disliked the German school system. At home, he studied science, math, and philosophy with the help of his Uncle Jakob, an engineer, and Max Talmud, a university student and family friend. His mother, a musician, made sure he learned the violin, which he played throughout his life.

EINSTEIN BECOMES A SWISS CITIZEN

After business problems, Einstein's father and uncle moved their families to Pavia, Italy, to start a new electrical engineering firm. They left Albert behind to finish high school. Not long afterward, Einstein talked a doctor into giving him a certificate that allowed him to be released from school. A few months before he turned sixteen, he joined his family in Italy and convinced his father to allow him to give up his German citizenship. This permitted him to avoid military service.

Einstein became a Swiss citizen in 1901. His parents sent him to a German-speaking school in Switzerland to prepare him for the Federal Institute of Technology. He entered the institute in 1896 thinking he would teach physics. Since he could not land a teaching job after graduation, Albert went to work in the Bern patent office in 1902. This easy job gave him time to explore scientific ideas he'd been thinking about for years.

HOW EINSTEIN'S 1905 PAPERS CHANGED THE WORLD

The first paper on the photoelectric effect confirmed that light interacts with matter as particles and not as waves—in what Max Planck called energy "packets" or "quanta."

The second paper argued that Brownian motion—in which particles suspended in a liquid appear to move at random—proves molecular action and the existence of atoms. This movement occurs because molecules of various sizes push the particles.

The third paper on the special theory of relativity stated that the speed of light (186,000 miles [299,338 km] per second) never changes relative to the speed of an observer or any other body in motion. It introduced the idea of spacetime (rather than two dimensions of space and time).

The fourth paper on mass-energy equivalence introduced the formula $E = mc2$, which predicted that very little mass could be converted into very large amounts of energy. This formula opened the door to the development of nuclear power, which splits the atom for that very purpose.

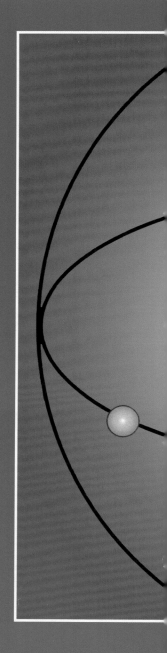

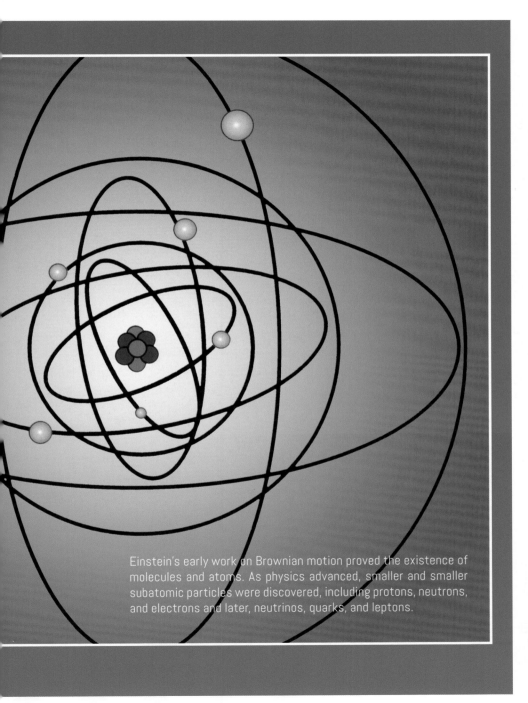

Einstein's early work on Brownian motion proved the existence of molecules and atoms. As physics advanced, smaller and smaller subatomic particles were discovered, including protons, neutrons, and electrons and later, neutrinos, quarks, and leptons.

EINSTEIN'S THEORIES MAKE HIM FAMOUS

The year 1905 has been called Einstein's year of miracles. That year, he wrote four important papers that changed physics. He also completed his PhD thesis on molecular dimension. About a decade later, he followed up his special relativity paper with a paper on general relativity. It explained that gravity is a force that bends spacetime. Astronomers in England tested and proved this theory in 1919. They observed the bending of starlight during a solar eclipse.

Once the scientific community caught up with Einstein's theories, he became famous. Many universities wanted to hire him. But Einstein's anti-war and pro-human beliefs put him at odds with German militancy and nationalism, which were on the rise after World War I. His politics along with his Jewish heritage would eventually make him an outsider in Germany. But in 1922, when Einstein won the Nobel Prize in Physics for his work on the photoelectric effect, the Germans eagerly claimed him. He taught at the University of Berlin and continued to maintain his Swiss citizenship, despite the fact that the Germans had once again made him a citizen.

EINSTEIN MOVES TO THE UNITED STATES

Einstein watched the start of fascism in Germany and left for good in 1932. Germany declared him an enemy of the state in 1933, the same year he began working at Princeton University in New Jersey. Congress agreed in 1934 to make Einstein an American citizen, but he chose to go through the citizenship process like everyone else. He became a permanent resident of the United States in 1935 and received citizenship in 1940. He also kept his Swiss citizenship.

Later in his career, Einstein hoped to create a "grand unified theory" to join together the insights of quantum mechanics

Franklin Delano Roosevelt had been in the White House for twelve years when he died—while serving his fourth term. Afterward, an amendment to the US Constitution was passed limiting the president's tenure to two terms of office.

(addressing the behavior of atomic particles) and relativity (addressing celestial bodies). The two theories were at odds. Quantum theory introduced paradoxical events. For example, depending on how one looks at light, it can appear as either a particle or a wave. Quantum theory grew out of Einstein's own work as well as that of Max Planck, the father of quantum mechanics. Quantum paradoxes bothered Einstein, and he debated them with Niels Bohr. These conversations put the paradoxes of quantum theory on solid ground, and Einstein had to live with that.

LETTER TO ROOSEVELT

In 1939, Einstein wrote a letter to President Franklin Roosevelt that later led the United States to make the first atomic bomb. Physicists Leo Szilárd and Eugene Wigner urged Einstein to speak for scientists who feared the outcome if Germany made an atomic weapon before the British or the Americans. Roosevelt took Einstein's words very seriously. He gave the green light to getting a group of physicists and engineers to work on the bomb.

The government recruited both Szilárd and Wigner for the project but didn't use Einstein. FBI director J. Edgar Hoover thought he was a communist because of his antiwar and antiracism stances. Einstein called racism "a disease of white people"[1] and helped African American actor Paul Robeson organize an antilynching campaign in 1946.

At the end of 1945, Einstein announced, "The war is won but the peace is not." From the end of the war until his death in 1955 at the age of seventy-six, Einstein took part in antinuclear activism. He called for a freeze on weapons he feared would destroy the world. He died of an abdominal aortic aneurysm, after refusing surgery to prolong his life. His son, engineer Hans Albert Einstein, and his stepdaughter, sculptor Margot Einstein, were with him in his final days, as was his assistant, Helen Dukas.

Italian-born Enrico Fermi was the first man to create a nuclear reactor and, along with Robert Oppenheimer, was instrumental in building the first atomic bombs, which were dropped on Hiroshima and Nagasaki, Japan, to quickly end World War II.

ENRICO FERMI AND THE MANHATTAN PROJECT

Enrico Fermi was a brilliant physicist. He worked as well in the lab as he did with a pencil and paper, figuring out the secrets of matter. Many consider him to be the "architect" of the atom bomb.

Born in Rome, Italy, on September 29, 1901, Enrico liked physics as a teen. He studied on his own as well as at school. Fermi also had a great memory. Adolfo Amidei, a friend of Enrico's father, mentored him by lending him books on math and mechanics.

Enrico began university training at the age of seventeen. He enrolled in the prestigious Scuola Normale Superior and at the University of Pisa, where he earned a doctorate in physics in 1922. He pursued postdoctoral work abroad and served as chair of a new theoretical physics department at the University of Rome in 1926.

FERMI ACCIDENTALLY STUMBLES ON FISSION

In 1932, Fermi provided mathematical evidence for the existence of an atomic particle. He named it "neutrino" to set it apart from neutrons. With a team, he studied the effects of bombarding alpha particles with neutrons to create artificial radioactivity in some elements. He then learned that slowing down neutrons leads to higher levels of radioactivity during bombardment.

He received the Nobel Prize in Physics in 1938 for his work. Fermi thought that the byproducts of these experiments had produced new elements. After receiving the Nobel Prize, he realized he'd actually split uranium atoms through fission. German scientists

Otto Hahn, Lise Meitner, and Fritz Strassmann had discovered fission in the same year.

Meanwhile, dictator Benito Mussolini put into place the same kinds of anti-Jewish laws in Italy that existed in Germany. Fermi had a Jewish wife and knew it was time to leave home. He had already made several trips to the United States and received invitations to teach and do research. After Fermi and his family traveled to Stockholm, Sweden, in 1938 to accept the Nobel Prize, they left for the United States on a temporary visa. They planned to become permanent US residents. Fermi didn't return to Italy until well after the war.

THE MANHATTAN PROJECT

President Roosevelt responded to Einstein's letter on the need to develop a nuclear weapon before the Germans did by setting up an advisory committee on uranium in October 1939. He also funded Fermi and Szilárd's first experiments at Columbia University the next year. Since the project began in New York City, officials called it the Manhattan Project. They assigned it to Colonel Leslie Richard Groves of the Army Corps of Engineers in September 1942. He hired an American physicist, J. Robert Oppenheimer, to head up the program. Together they chose the site of a failing school in Los Alamos, New Mexico, as headquarters for the atom-bomb project and recruited the best scientists available.

Enrico Fermi was one of several immigrants who worked on the Manhattan Project. Others included:

(continued on the next page)

(continued from the previous page)

- Maria Goeppert Mayer, a German American immigrant, worked in New York and Los Alamos and later earned a 1963 Nobel Prize in Physics for proposing the nuclear shell model of the atom's nucleus.
- Chien Shiung Wu, a Chinese American, worked with Fermi at Columbia to develop weapons-grade uranium.
- Hans Bethe, a German Jewish refugee, headed the theoretical physics division at Los Alamos. He won the 1967 Nobel Prize in Physics for his work on energy production in stars.
- James Franck, a German Jewish refugee, and Eugene Wigner, a Hungarian Jewish refugee, worked in Chicago. Wigner helped design the nuclear reactors and later shared the 1963 Nobel Prize in Physics with Mayer and Jensen.
- Edward Teller, a Hungarian Jewish refugee, worked at Los Alamos; later, he and Stanislaw Ulam designed the hydrogen bomb.
- Leo Szilrd, a Hungarian Jewish refugee, worked with Fermi on the first nuclear "piles" in New York and Chicago. He objected to the use of the weapon on the Japanese, but the government ignored his concerns.

FERMI AND THE ATOMIC BOMB

When Fermi arrived in the United States, he accepted a position at Columbia University in New York. Within weeks of his arrival, the physics community discussed fission's significance. Fermi worked with Leo Szilárd to create an early nuclear reaction using fission. After the United States entered the war in 1941, Fermi moved to the

The Trinity Test exploded the first atomic bomb at Alamogordo, New Mexico, on July 16, 1945. The bomb was detonated on a steel tower and produced an intense flash of light and a mushroom cloud 40,000 feet (12,192 meters) wide.

47

University of Chicago. By the end of 1942, he created a reactor "pile" that he could start, control, and stop.

Over the next two years, he continued this work in Chicago with the help of the American government. He visited Oak Ridge, Tennessee, and Hanford, Washington, where nuclear reactors made the plutonium needed for the atomic bomb. In 1944, Fermi and his wife became US citizens and moved to Los Alamos, New Mexico. There, scientists worked to create the physical bomb. He oversaw the experimental physics department, watching the first bomb test on July 16, 1945.

Fermi also served as a scientific consultant to President Truman's advisory committee that decided to use the bomb for military purposes. The United States dropped the first and only atomic bombs on the Japanese cities of Hiroshima and Nagasaki in August 1945. The Japanese surrendered on August 15, which ended the war in the Pacific. The bomb killed about 80,000 people immediately in Hiroshima and 135,000 people total, in a city with a population of 255,000. The bomb killed about 50,000 people in Nagasaki, a city of 195,000 people. Many survivors suffered long-term health problems that stemmed from radiation burns and poisoning.

After the war ended, Fermi went back to the University of Chicago to lead a new generation of physicists. He also turned his attention to elementary particle physics. He continued to advise the Atomic Energy Commission, and he spoke out against the creation of thermonuclear and hydrogen bombs. Still, he returned to Los Alamos to help create these weapons.

Fermi died of stomach cancer in 1954 at the age of fifty-three.

CHAPTER 4

IMMIGRANTS IN MEDICINE

I mmigrant physicians to the United States have made important contributions to health care for the past century. Gerty Theresa Cori won the Nobel Prize in Physiology or Medicine for her work on sugar metabolism, and Elias Zerhouni more recently has improved the quality of magnetic resonance technology.

GERTY THERESA CORI

Gerty Theresa Radnitz Cori was the third woman to win a Nobel Prize and the first American woman to do so. She won in 1947 for her work with her husband, Carl Cori, on the breakdown of glucose, or sugar. Researchers have used the couple's work to better understand and treat diabetes.

Gerty Theresa Radnitz was born in Prague on August 15, 1896. The oldest of three girls, Gerty's father was a chemist and manager of sugar-beet factories. Gerty was first taught by private tutors. She then attended a private girls' school, but she wanted to become a physician. Given the difference in boys' and girls' education, she had to prepare for medical school by taking extra classes in math, science, and Latin. At the age of eighteen, she passed the tests needed to enter medical school at the German University of Prague in 1914.

Prague-born Gerty and Carl Cori won the 1947 Nobel Prize for medicine for their work linking phosphates, glucose, and metabolism. The Cori lab went on to do pioneering work in enzymes and produced six other Nobel Prize winners.

At school, she met her future husband. Raised in the Jewish religion, she converted to Roman Catholicism for him. The couple married in 1920, but her husband's anti-Semitic family opposed the match. Anti-Semitism began to spread after World War I, and the Coris left Europe and moved to America.

THE CORI CYCLE

After graduation, Cori worked as an assistant in a children's hospital in Vienna. There, she studied and wrote papers on thyroid deficiency. From early in her career, Cori suffered gender discrimination. In 1922, her husband accepted a biochemistry position at the State Institute for the Study of Malignant Diseases (now called Roswell Park Memorial Institute), in Buffalo, New York. Cori followed, taking a lower level position as an assistant pathologist, although she had the same training and experience as her husband. The Coris worked in different departments but found ways to team up. In 1928, the couple became US citizens.

The Coris wanted to learn how the body metabolizes, or breaks down, glucose. Sugar metabolism is the basis for all life activities. Glycogen (a starchy substance) had been discovered in the nineteenth century. Scientists knew that poor sugar metabolism could lead to diabetes and that insulin kept sugar in check. But they did not understand how insulin worked or how the body metabolized carbohydrates. In 1929, the Coris published their findings on the lactic acid cycle, which explained how the body creates energy through chemical processes in the muscles and liver.

In 1931, Cori and her husband moved to the Washington University School of Medicine in St. Louis, Missouri. Her husband chaired the pharmacology department, while Cori worked as a researcher. When the couple moved to the biological chemistry department, Cori became an associate professor. In 1947, the university promoted her to professor. Just a few months later, she won the Nobel Prize in Physiology or Medicine. The Coris won the prize in medicine for discovering the catalytic conversion of glycogen. Unfortunately, Cori developed bone marrow disease the same year, possibly as a result of her previous work with X-rays.

THE CORI CYCLE (LACTIC ACID CYCLE)

The Coris found an intermediate stage of glycogen breakdown into a form of glucose, now known as the "Cori ester." They also discovered the enzyme (phosphorylase) that started this reaction. The catalyzed glycogen provided the cells with immediate energy.

Insulin helps to create glycogen in muscles and the liver, while epinephrine decreases glycogen. After the body breaks down glycogen to ATP (adenosine triphosphate) and other molecules, traces of lactic acid remain. ATP is the only molecule that cells can use to do their work. The body recycles lactic acid, which builds up during muscle activity and sends it back to the liver. There, it is converted into glycogen, which the muscles can use again.

This is a continuous chemical cycle of the build-up and breakdown of molecules to produce ATP, which fuels the cells. The Cori cycle became important in understanding and treating diabetes. The disease occurs when the body has trouble making or using insulin. This problem leads to high blood sugar levels in the body.

ENZYME RESEARCH

Although Cori received many awards, she also lost out on many career opportunities, probably because she was a woman. In the late 1930s, the Coris focused on enzyme research and discovered phosphorylase, which breaks down glycogen. The couple found a number of other enzymes as well. By 1947, the Cori lab became famous. Researchers, including six Nobel Prize winners, visited the lab.

Despite her illness, Cori continued to work full-time in the lab. She studied glycogen storage diseases and become a pioneer in the field of genetic diseases. Cori published her last article in 1957. By then, her husband had to carry her around the lab. Kept in bed for a month, she died on October 26, 1957. Her husband lived until his eighties. The couple had a son who studied chemistry and became president of a chemical company.

ELIAS ZERHOUNI

Elias Zerhouni is a leader in the field of radiology. He developed new imaging techniques for diagnosing cancer and heart disease. He also served as director of the National Institutes of Health from 2002 to 2008, under President George W. Bush.

Elias Zerhouni was born on April 12, 1951, in Nedroma, Algeria. The family moved to Algiers when Elias was two years old. Since his father was a math and physics teacher, the family of nine belonged to the middle class and enjoyed a better quality of life than most North Africans. The people of Algeria, mostly Arab and Muslim, won independence from the French in 1962. The war against the French didn't stop Elias from attending school and competing on the national swim team. He earned his medical degree from the University of Algiers in 1975 and decided to move, along with his wife, to the United States where there would be more career opportunities.

53

Algerian-born Elias Zerhouni, president of global research and development at the French pharmaceutical company Sanofi, served as the director of the US National Institutes of Health from 2002 to 2008 and tackled conflict of interest issues among NIH scientists during his tenure.

Zerhouni began a residency in radiology at Johns Hopkins University in Baltimore, Maryland. Four years later, he became an assistant professor at the university's medical school. He later became a professor in the radiology department. He also served as a vice dean at the Johns Hopkins School of Medicine and as dean of research and clinical affairs.

PIONEER IN MAGNETIC RESONANCE IMAGING

Zerhouni is a doctor as well as a scientist and inventor. He is a world expert in magnetic resonance imaging (MRI) and extended the use of MRI beyond simply taking pictures of the anatomy to visualizing the body at the molecular level.

He "pioneered magnetic tagging, a non-invasive method of using MRI to track the motions of a heart in three dimensions," according to the National Institutes of Health. "He is also renowned for refining an imaging technique called computer tomographic (CT) densitometry that helps discriminate between non-cancerous and cancerous nodules in the lung."[1]

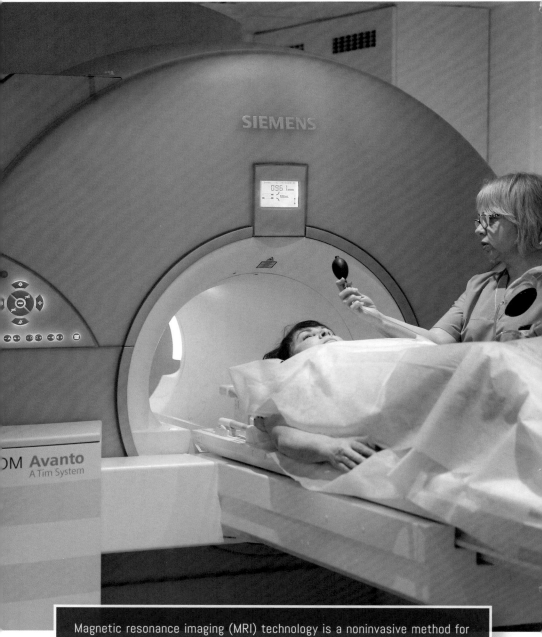

Magnetic resonance imaging (MRI) technology is a noninvasive method for producing three-dimensional, detailed anatomical images without using radiation from X-rays. MRI scanners use magnetic fields and radio waves to create pictures of what is going on in the body.

Zerhouni has received eight patents based on this work and has started imaging and radiology companies. This immigrant who came to the United States with less than $400 is now a multimillionaire. Zerhouni served as a consultant to the White House in 1985 and to the World Health Organization in 1988. He became a US citizen in 1990.

NIH DIRECTOR

In 2002, Zerhouni became director of the National Institutes of Health (NIH). Soon after, he started the NIH's Roadmap for Medical Research to find opportunities and gaps in biomedical research. Zerhouni also encouraged the many NIH departments to work together on common projects. In addition, he started The Strategic Plan for NIH Obesity Research, which called for research that looked at genetic, behavioral, and environmental causes of obesity.

Because of Zerhouni, the NIH began a new public-access policy that allowed people to use the internet to read NIH research. But Zerhouni has also raised controversy, such as in 2005, when he banned NIH scientists from advising drug and device companies. He made the move after a congressional investigation found scientists were mixing their government jobs with outside consulting deals.

NATIONAL INSTITUTES OF HEALTH

The National Institutes of Health, operating under the US Department of Health and Human Services, is the largest biomedical agency in the world. The NIH includes twenty-seven institutes or Centers. The NIH began in 1887 as a one-room laboratory in the Marine Hospital Service (MHS) for the medical care of merchant seamen. By the 1880s, the MHS was examining immigrants arriving from other countries to spot signs of infectious diseases. The MHS later became the Public Health Service, and new laws led to the opening of the National Institute of Health in 1930. In 1948, it became the National Institutes of Health.

The NIH's mission is to encourage new discoveries in medicine that will improve health and to provide resources to do so. The agency also promotes scientific honesty and public responsibility. NIH spends about $32 billion yearly on medical research. About 10 percent of its budget funds about 6,000 scientists at NIH labs, mostly on its own campus.[2]

Zerhouni resigned from the NIH in 2008. The next year, he served as a presidential science representative for President Barack Obama. In this role, he worked to get the US and other countries to work together in the sciences. He also served as a senior fellow at the Bill & Melinda Gates Foundation from 2009 to 2010. Then, pharmaceutical company Sanofi hired him to lead their global research and development department. This division of Sanofi makes both medicines and vaccines.

Zerhouni later returned to Johns Hopkins as a professor and senior advisor. He has three children with his wife Nadia, a pediatrician.

CHAPTER 5

IMMIGRANT BIOLOGISTS

E lizabeth Blackburn's genetic research helped scientists better understand the factors that lead to a long life. Gebisa Ejeta used his knowledge of genetics to improve the crop for Africa's second most important cereal. Both were immigrants. Learn more about their amazing contributions to the science world.

ELIZABETH BLACKBURN

Elizabeth Blackburn is an Australian American molecular biologist who has become well known for her work on telomeres and their connection to health. Blackburn, along with Carol W. Greider and Jack Szostak, won the 2009 Nobel Prize in Physiology or Medicine for discovering how telomeres protect chromosomes as well as the enzyme telomerase. The enzyme plays a key role in the upkeep of telomeres.

Blackburn became a US citizen in September 2003. She chairs the microbiology and immunology department at the University of California, San Francisco.

Born on November 26, 1948, in Hobart, Tasmania, Elizabeth Blackburn was the second oldest of seven children. Her parents were physicians, as were an aunt and uncle. Given the strong interest

An Australian by birth, Elizabeth Blackburn was inducted into the California Hall of Fame in 2011. Blackburn, now a Californian, won the Nobel Prize in Medicine in 2009, along with Carol Greider and Jack Szostak, for discovering how telomeres protect chromosomes.

in science in Elizabeth's family, which also included geologists and a minister who practiced botany, she enjoyed nature and science at an early age. As a child, she lived in a farm town and had access to animals and other creatures at home and near the sea. She began taking advanced science classes in elementary school. Although she had an interest in music, "nobility of the scientific quest"[1] attracted her more, according to the biography she wrote for the Nobel committee.

She looked up to Marie Curie, a Polish-French physicist. Curie stands out as the first woman to win a Nobel Prize. She was also the only person to win a Nobel in two different sciences (physics and chemistry).

When Elizabeth was in her last year of high school, her family moved to Melbourne, Australia. She entered the University of Melbourne as a biochemistry major, graduating with an honors degree. She continued with master's level work in the research laboratory, investigating amino acid metabolism. During this period, her advisor, Frank Hird, introduced her to Fred Sanger. Soon afterward, she enrolled as a PhD student at Cambridge University's MRC Laboratory of Molecular Biology under Sanger's watch. Sanger had won a Nobel Prize in Chemistry, and Blackburn worked on genetic sequencing in his lab to earn her PhD. At the Cambridge lab, Blackburn also met her future husband, John Sedat. The couple traveled to Yale University in New Haven, Connecticut, to do postdoctoral research.

At Yale, Blackburn investigated the chromosomes of a *Tetrahymena* protozoan (a single-celled, microscopic animal). By sequencing the ends (telomeres) of the tiny animal's DNA strand, she learned that telomeres are made of short, repeating segments of DNA subunits.

WHAT ARE TELOMERES?

Telomeres are structures at the end of chromosomes that act as protective "caps" to preserve genetic information. In the 1930s, geneticists Barbara McClintock and Herman Muller realized that telomeres (named by Muller) protected the integrity of the DNA on the chromosome string. Telomeres work similarly to the protective plastic tips at the ends of shoelaces.

In the early 1960s, biologist Leonard Hayflick proposed that a normal cell in mitosis (non-sexual cell reproduction) can reproduce itself or divide between forty and sixty times before it eventually dies, which went against the leading theory that cells were immortal (could infinitely replicate themselves). A Russian biologist, Alexey Olovnikov, proposed in the early 1970s that the ends of chromosomes do not replicate when a cell divides. He believed that DNA subunits on the telomere are lost every time a cell replicates, until the cell's telomeres become too short for the cell to reproduce.

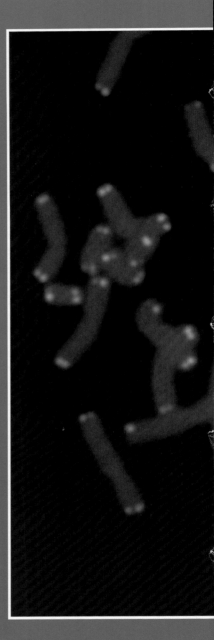

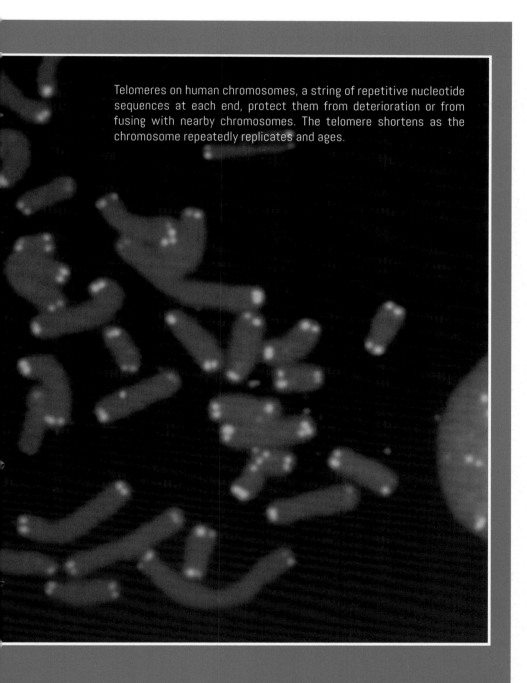

Telomeres on human chromosomes, a string of repetitive nucleotide sequences at each end, protect them from deterioration or from fusing with nearby chromosomes. The telomere shortens as the chromosome repeatedly replicates and ages.

In the late 1970s, she and Sedat moved to California, where Blackburn became an associate professor in molecular biology at the University of California, Berkeley. There, she continued her research on telomeres. In 1986, Blackburn and her husband had their son, Ben. By 1990, Blackburn moved to the University of California, San Francisco, where her husband had worked since the couple moved to the Bay Area.

By the early 1980s, Blackburn and her researchers realized that the number of repeating chromosomal subunits in telomeres was not alike. They varied, not only by organism, but also by cells within one organism, and they could change over time. The telomere could get shorter or longer. This suggested that an enzyme must be at work. Enzymes are catalysts in cells that spur biochemical reactions.

FINDING TELOMERASE

In 1984, Blackburn and Carol Greider discovered telomerase, an enzyme that helps add more subunits to a telomere. In 1988, Greider, Calvin Harley, and their partner researchers found out in the lab that Olovnikov was right. Most normal human cells lost parts of their telomeres during cell division when not in the presence of telomerase. They made a strong connection between aging and shortening telomeres.

Research through the 1990s found that telomerase is active in some types of cancer, although it appears to become active after bad cells have already gone rogue. This shows that telomerase doesn't cause the cancer—it just helps it survive. The finding suggests new directions for cancer research. For example, new drugs might target telomerase in cancer cells and turn it off.

Blackburn began to make links between telomere shortening and the presence or absence of telomerase and medical problems. For example, she and psychologist Elissa Epel worked on research of people suffering long-term stress. They found that these people had shorter telomeres and fewer telomerase than those who had not suffered long-term stress. She also has studied the possible effects of body-mind techniques like meditation on the production of telomerase.

According to Blackburn, telomeres can be protected and perhaps even lengthened (in the presence of telomerase) with regular exercise, a healthy diet, proper sleep, and control of emotional stress. Blackburn sees a clear connection between the aging process and ability of telomeres to add new parts to cells, although some scientists question this. Blackburn's work in this fascinating field of biology may very well offer more findings in the future.

GEBISA EJETA

Gebisa Ejeta has lived in the United States since 1974. He became a 2009 World Food Prize Laureate for his work on sorghum hybrid plants for both the American and world markets. Sorghum is a kind of cereal.

Born in 1950, Gebisa Ejeta grew up in the Ethiopian farm town of Wollonkomi. According to his biography on The World Food Prize website, Gebisa's mother made sure her son got the best education available. That meant he attended school more than 12 miles (19.3 km) from home. Gebisa walked back and forth from school at the beginning and end of the school week through his first eight grades.[2] He completed his secondary education at Jimma Agricultural and Technical School and then entered Alemaya College in Eastern Ethiopia. He received a bachelor's degree in plant science from the college in 1973.

That year, he also met a sorghum researcher from Purdue University (located in West Lafayette, Indiana). The researcher

Born in Ethiopia, Gebisa Ejeta (*left*, pictured with Microsoft founder Bill Gates) won the 2009 World Food Prize for his work on sorghum hybrid plants that could more easily resist drought and the deadly weed *Striga*.

invited him to the United States to do graduate work. Ejeta began his graduate work in 1974, completing a PhD in plant breeding and genetics. He then took a job as a sorghum researcher at the International Crop Research Institute for the Semi-Arid Tropics office in Sudan.

HOW EJETA CHANGED SORGHUM

While in the Sudan, Ejeta developed sorghum plants that could tolerate drought and produce more grain than current crops. These new hybrids, released in 1983, significantly increased the harvest and started a commercial sorghum seed industry in Sudan. As part of his work to help poor farmers rise out of poverty, Ejeta has spoken out about the production and marketing of the hybrid seed, as well as soil and water conservation and other good crop-management practices. He developed another drought-tolerant plant for Niger with one of his graduate students in 1992,

While sorghum is fed to livestock in the United States, it is a dietary staple of thirty countries with a limited food supply. Sorghum has twenty-two grams of protein per cooked cup and is rich in antioxidants.

which produced four to five times more than the national average of sorghum in that country. He then developed more than seventy lines of sorghum for markets in the United States and abroad.

In the 1990s, he tackled the deadly weed *Striga* (witchweed), a parasitic plant that destroys sorghum as well as other crops. Ejeta and his colleague, Larry Butler, developed a new approach to get rid of *Striga*. They found genes for *Striga* resistance and put them in local plants. This new sorghum could be adapted to different farming conditions in Africa. In 1994, the *Striga*-resistant plants entered the market in twelve African countries. They have produced four times more sorghum than local plants that have not been changed genetically. A second effort, from 2002 to 2003, introduced the weed-resistant plants in three more countries, along with a *Striga*-management program that added fertilization and water conservation to harvesting practices. This effort increased productivity even more. In 2009, Ejeta received the World Food Prize for his groundbreaking work in increasing crop yields for sorghum.

WHAT IS SORGHUM?

Sorghum comes from northeastern Africa. It probably first appeared about ten thousand years ago. It made its way to other continents more recently. Today, sorghum is one of the top five cereals in the world. A cereal is a grass that is grown for the parts of its grain that can be eaten. Sorghum grain can be eaten by people or animals, and sweet sorghum is used to make syrup.

The United States produces more sorghum than any other country—close to six hundred million bushels in 2015. But American sorghum is mostly used to feed livestock that the public will eat.[3] The United States sends sorghum to other countries for the same reason. Scientists are also exploring using sorghum to make ethanol, or alcohol, as well as nonfood items.

Sorghum is a major part of the diet for more than five hundred million people in thirty countries, according to South Africa's Department of Agriculture, Forestry and Fisheries.[4] Sorghum is Africa's second most important cereal, and the continent produces about twenty million tons per year. This makes up about a third of the world's total.[5] The crop is a key food for people with a limited food supply, and production of sorghum in Africa has been rising.

Sorghum is adapted to Africa's climate. It is naturally drought resistant and able to withstand flooding. It is used in foods such as bread, couscous, dumplings, and porridges. It is also used to make traditional beers. Sorghum often appears in vegetable oils, adhesives, waxes, and dyes. According to Worldwatch Institute, "Dr. Ejeta's hybrids have dramatically increased production of sorghum and made it a more viable food crop for millions of people in sub-Saharan Africa."[6]

Ejeta's work to increase crop yields has positively affected food security in Africa. His efforts to promote wealth in Africa and give small farmers there more power have positively affected the lives of many people. The author of more than two hundred scientific papers, Ejeta continues to teach at Purdue and lead research on African agricultural development. He is Purdue's distinguished professor of plant breeding and genetics and international agriculture. He also serves as executive director of the Purdue Center for Global Food Security. He is a fellow of the American Association for the Advancement of Science as well as of the Crop Science Society of America and the American Society of Agronomy. He has also received a national medal of honor from the president of Ethiopia. In 2011, President Barack Obama named him to the International Food and Agricultural Development board.

CHAPTER 6

IMMIGRANT ASTRONAUTS

Both Franklin Chang-Díaz and Kalpana Chalwa came to the United States with hopes of becoming astronauts. Learn how these two immigrants achieved their dreams.

FRANKLIN CHANG-DÍAZ

Franklin Chang-Díaz came to the United States as a teenager with the goal of later working for the National Aeronautics Space Administration (NASA). He has been called the first Hispanic American in space (although he has Chinese heritage, too). He is also one of just two astronauts ever to have made seven space voyages.

Chang-Díaz was born on April 5, 1950, in San José, Costa Rica. He grew up one of six children. His father, Ramón Ángel Chang-Morales, was an oil worker and son of a Chinese immigrant. His grandfather fled to Central America during China's Boxer Rebellion, a peasant uprising to drive foreigners out of the country. Franklin's mother, María Eugenia Díaz-Romero, was Costa Rican. At one point, Franklin's father moved the family to Venezuela, where Franklin attended elementary school.

Costa Rican-born Franklin Chang-Díaz went into space seven times, and after retiring from the National Aeronautics and Space Administration, started his own company to work on advanced rocket propulsion systems for longer space flights.

FIRST STEPS: COMING TO AMERICA

As a child, Franklin took an interest in space travel. The first satellite, Sputnik, launched by the Russians in 1957, fascinated him. He played space travel games with his friends, using a big cardboard box as a spaceship to imagine hopping from planet to planet. The young boy was also impressed with the launch of the first nuclear submarine, the USS *Nautilus*. The sub allowed for nonstop underwater travel.

At fifteen, Franklin built homemade rockets and even sent a mouse, wearing a special helmet, 100 feet (30.5 m) in the air. He wrote to Wernher von Braun, the head of NASA's rocket program, but later learned that one had to be American to work for NASA.[1] So, he graduated from high school and then moved to Hartford, Connecticut, where family members lived. He repeated his senior year of high school there in order to learn English. At first, he flunked his classes, but he soon began to do well in his American school.

One of his teachers mentored and coached him. This helped the young immigrant win a full engineering scholarship to the University of Connecticut. Chang-Díaz almost lost the scholarship when officials learned he was not a US citizen. His teachers convinced state lawmakers to let him keep the scholarship. In the end, he received a one-year scholarship. He worked at the university's physics department and took out loans to pay for the rest of his college years.

WORKING AT NASA

Chang-Díaz earned his bachelor's degree in mechanical engineering in 1973. From there, he went to the Massachusetts Institute of Technology (MIT) to study applied plasma physics. He researched controlled fusion for the design and operation of fusion nuclear reactors. Fusion energy from nuclear reactions releases much more energy than usual fission. It may also be a cleaner form of energy.

After becoming an American citizen and graduating from MIT in 1977 with a doctorate in applied plasma physics, Chang-Díaz worked at Charles Stark Draper Laboratory. There, he continued his fusion work. In 1979, he came up with a way to direct fusion pellets in a reaction chamber. He also worked on a new approach to rocket propulsion that involved high temperature plasmas.[2]

In May 1980, Chang-Díaz's life changed when NASA accepted him into its astronaut program. The following year, his childhood dream came true when he became an astronaut. From 1983 to 1993, Chang-Díaz also worked as a visiting scientist for MIT's Plasma Fusion Center. He led the plasma propulsion program that tried to create technology for human missions to Mars. According to NASA, Chang-Díaz was "instrumental in implementing closer ties between the astronaut corps and the scientific community."[3] He married Peggy Marguerite Doncaster in 1984, and the couple had four daughters.

From 1993 to 2005, Chang-Díaz led the Advanced Space Propulsion Laboratory at Johnson Space Center in Houston, Texas. After he retired from NASA, he started a business called Ad Astra Rocket Company to continue his work with rocket technology. The company is developing the Variable Specific Impulse Magnetoplasma Rocket (VASIMR), which may transform space travel. The VASIMR would be able to travel round-trip to the farthest parts of the solar system.

KALPANA CHAWLA

Kalpana Chawla, an Indian American aerospace engineer and astronaut, died in the *Columbia* shuttle disaster of 2003. Six others died as well. The Indian community proudly claimed her as the first Indian-born woman in space. But Chawla thought of herself as a "citizen of the world," according to her sister Sunita Chaudhary. She felt that she belonged everywhere. She became interested in space travel at an early age, according to her friends and family.[4]

SEVEN SPACE VOYAGES

Chang-Díaz's first space mission took place in 1986 on the *Columbia* shuttle. During this six-day flight, he helped to set up a satellite. In a 1989 flight, he was part of the crew of the space shuttle *Atlantis* that deployed the *Galileo* spacecraft to explore Jupiter. In 1992, once again aboard *Atlantis*, he participated in an eight-day mission to install the European Retrievable Carrier satellite and completed the first Tethered Satellite System (TSS) test flight.

His 1994 flight aboard the space shuttle *Discovery* was the first joint American-Russian space mission. He flew again in 1996, 1998, and 2002. His last mission on *Endeavour* delivered a new crew to the International Space Station, and Chang-Díaz performed three spacewalks to set up a Canadian-built mobile base for the space station's robotic arm. *Endeavour* also brought home the old crew, who had been in space for more than six months.

The *Columbia* was the first vehicle to launch in the space shuttle program in April 1981. The spacecraft served for twenty-two years and completed twenty-seven missions before tragically disintegrating during reentry on February 1, 2003, killing all seven crew members.

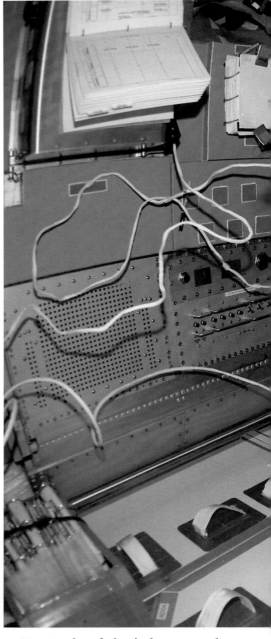

Kalpana Chawla was born on March 17, 1962, in Haryana, India. She was the youngest child of four and one of three daughters. The Chawlas were Sikhs, a religious minority group. Because of their religion, they were forced to move from Pakistan to India in 1947. At that time, the subcontinent divided into India and Pakistan. Muslims gathered in Pakistan, while Hindus and Sikhs lived in India. At first, Kalpana's family had very little, but her father, Barnarsi Lal, became a wealthy businessman in the rubber industry. Kalpana grew up in a community where women faced sexism, but her mother, Syongita, and eldest sister told her to follow her dreams.

THE ROAD TO NASA

Kalpana attended Tagore Baal Niketan Senior Secondary School and then Punjab Engineering College in Chandigarh. In 1982, she became the first woman to graduate with a degree in aeronautical engineering. Despite her father's disapproval, she then moved to the United States to attend the University of

Indian American astronaut Kalpana Chawla, mission specialist on the ill-fated *Columbia* space shuttle, died with her crew members sixteen minutes before the spacecraft was scheduled to land. Chawla continues to be a role model, especially for young Indian women.

Texas at Arlington. There, she earned a master's degree in aerospace engineering in 1984. After that, she moved to the University of Colorado, Boulder, to get another master's degree as well as a doctorate in aerospace engineering in 1988.

She married Jean-Pierre Harrison, a flight instructor, and learned how to fly. When she died, Chawla had a flight instructor's license that allowed her in the cockpit of several kinds of aircraft.

Chawla started working at NASA in 1988. She began research on powered-lift computational fluid dynamics at NASA's Ames Research Center. "Powered-lift" refers to aircraft that vertically take-off or land, while "computational fluid dynamics" refers to the data analysis of fluid flows. So, Chawla's work involved studying the air-flow patterns that take place around aircraft.

WHEN WOMEN SCIENTISTS WERE SIDELINED

In the early days of NASA, women encountered sexism. Men received recognition that women didn't. For example, female mathematicians, called computers, worked out the equations of NASA engineers who put the first rockets into space. Despite their obvious talents, NASA often treated such women like secretaries. One gifted black mathematician, Katherine Goble Johnson, calculated landing routes for John Glenn's orbit around Earth. She did the same for the historic moon landing in the 1960s. Women also worked in the Jet Propulsion Laboratory. But when the lab celebrated its fiftieth anniversary of the first American satellite, they were not on the invitation list.

Sexism played out in other science fields as well. Lise Meitner, a Hungarian Jew who fled to Sweden during the Holocaust, worked with two male physicists on nuclear fission. Her partner, Otto Hahn, won the 1944 Nobel Prize in Chemistry, but she did not. And English chemist Rosalind Franklin produced X-ray images of DNA that led to the discovery of its double-helix structure. Scientists James Watson, Francis Crick, and Maurice Wilkins shared the 1962 Nobel Prize in Physiology or Medicine for this discovery, while Franklin was overlooked.

Katherine Johnson, a NASA mathematician and African American woman, received the Presidential Medal of Freedom from Barack Obama in 2015 for her contributions to early space flights.

BECOMING AN ASTRONAUT

Chalwa became an American citizen in 1991 and applied for astronaut training. NASA, however, did not select her for the program until the end of 1994. The previous year, she became vice president and research scientist for a Los Altos, California, company that solved aerodynamic problems. Research papers and journals mentioned the results of different projects she took part in, according to her NASA biography.[5]

Chawla began training as an astronaut in March 1995. By then, she had made up with her family, who took pride in her accomplishments. In November 1996, Chawla became a mission specialist and robotic arm operator for the *Columbia* space shuttle's twenty-fourth flight. She flew her first mission at the end of 1997. The astronauts on this flight studied how weightlessness affects physical processes. They also observed the sun's outer layers.

Chawla asked NASA to invite her high school in India to the summer space program that the International Space School Foundation in Houston sponsored. Starting in 1998, two students from India spent several weeks in Houston every year. Chawla would serve them dinners of home-cooked Indian food.

Sadly, Chawla's second mission turned out to be the last for her and the *Columbia* space shuttle. The sixteen-day mission, which began on January 16, 2003, had rotating crews working nonstop to perform eighty experiments. The February 1 return flight of the *Columbia* ended sixteen minutes before it should have landed. The spacecraft broke apart, and the seven astronauts aboard died.

After her death, Chawla received the Congressional Space Medal of Honor, the NASA Space Flight Medal, and the Distinguished Service Medal for her service and bravery.

WHAT HAPPENED TO *COLUMBIA*?

NASA officials didn't tell Kalpana Chawla and her fellow crew members that they might die during reentry. The crew included Rick Husband, Michael Anderson, David Brown, Laurel Clark, William McCool, and Ilan Ramon. The people on the ground thought the shuttle might have been seriously damaged during takeoff. Flight director John Harpold said that nothing could be done for a damaged thermal protection system.

(continued on the next page)

The crew of NASA space shuttle mission STS-107 who died in the *Columbia* disaster included (*from left to right*) Kalpana Chawla, Laurel Clark, pilot William "Willie" McCool, Commander Rick Husband, David Brown, Ilan Ramon, and Michael Anderson.

(continued from the previous page)

NASA decided it was better for the crew not to know what happened. Also, some NASA officials wanted to get pictures of the damaged wing while *Columbia* was orbiting, which the Department of Defense's spy satellites could have taken. However, NASA officials in charge of the mission turned down the offer, according to the *Columbia* Accident Investigation Board. The board released a report in August 2003.

The board reported that a piece of foam, about the size of a briefcase, had smashed into the shuttle's left wing during takeoff. It knocked off some of the protective tiles. The accident created a hole in the left wing that allowed gases to seep into the shuttle during reentry. On February 1, the shuttle showed abnormal readings before it was supposed to land. The ground crew lost communication with the astronauts, and the spacecraft broke apart at 9 a.m.

In 2008, NASA released a report that said the astronauts probably survived the initial breakup of the shuttle but blacked out seconds after the cabin pressure dropped. They likely died as the shuttle broke apart. The search for debris from the wreckage covered 2,000 square miles (3,219 km). NASA ended up recovering about 40 percent of *Columbia*. Officials identified the crew with DNA tests.

The *Columbia* Accident Investigation Board blamed NASA for ignoring safety problems. NASA took care of these problems during future space flights. In 2011, NASA's space shuttle program ended.

When astronauts go on shuttle missions, they have a chance to speak with their families. On Kalpana's last flight, she told her mother, "I saw my reflection in the window [of the spacecraft], and I could see my eyes and the retinas of my eyes … I could see the whole earth in the retinas."

Chawla felt lucky to have achieved her dreams. She remains an inspiration to many, especially Indian girls. India named its first weather satellite Kalpana 1, and a planetarium in Kurukshetra, India, also bears her name. After the *Columbia* accident, a portion of 74th Street in Jackson Heights, New York, was renamed Kalpana Chawla Way. The area is home to a large South Asian community.

CHAPTER 7

IMMIGRANTS AT THE FRONTIERS OF SCIENCE AND TECHNOLOGY

Migration has been a fact of life from the earliest days of humanity. People began to head to North America tens of thousands of years ago. The individuals who created the United States arrived some four hundred years ago. The new country, established in 1776, housed a mixture of immigrants, Native Americans, and enslaved West Africans. As the United States grew, it became more and more diverse.

By the twentieth century, America had become a "melting pot." The now-forgotten playwright, Israel Zangwill, gave the country this nickname in 1908. He wanted to show that the many people who came to US shores from other lands could become great Americans. Later, the term came to mean that the United States is a country with endless multicolored strands quilted together in one republic.

Today, many people of color prefer the term "salad bowl" to "melting pot." That's because in a melting pot the ingredients lose their flavor and uniqueness.

Anyone without recent ancestors from Africa has some Neanderthal DNA, since these earlier humans mated with their modern cousins when they arrived in Europe and Asia. Most Europeans and Asians have 1 to 2 percent Neanderthal DNA.

But the ingredients that make up a salad remain distinct from each other. People who take pride in their ethnic heritage may enjoy living in a country with many different kinds of individuals, but they don't necessarily want to blend in with everyone else.

In February 1942, President Roosevelt ordered all ethnic Japanese (about two-thirds of whom were Americans) to evacuate the West Coast and report to internment camps. No comparable order applied to Japanese Americans in Hawaii or to German or Italian Americans.

INCLUSIVENESS VERSUS XENOPHOBIA

While the melting pot is a beautiful American story, it may be somewhat of a fairy tale. Throughout its history, the United States has both embraced immigrants and rejected them. Often, the skin color and national origins of immigrants drive their experiences in the United States.

Evidence of rejection includes the Chinese Exclusion Act of 1882 and the Immigration Acts of 1917 and 1924. These laws barred immigration from the Asia-Pacific region and created quotas that favored "Nordic" Europeans.

President Roosevelt's Executive Order 9066, which forced Japanese Americans into internment camps during World War II, stands out as another example of xenophobia, or fear of foreigners, in the United States. On the other hand, the Immigration and Nationality Act of 1965 did away with racist quotas and opened the door to Asian immigrants. Also, the US Refugee Act of 1980 admitted millions of refugees, and the Immigration

Reform and Control Act of 1986 paved the way to citizenship for three million undocumented immigrants. The Immigration Act of 1990 notably increased employment-based green cards.

No one theory explains why people fear immigrants. Some scientists claim that it's human nature for people to protect their territory and dislike people different from them. But many people disagree with such theories. After all, many of the Native Americans who greeted Columbus and his crew welcomed the explorers. Little did they know that Columbus viewed them as inferior and wanted their land.

Some psychologists and social scientists blame xenophobia on nationalism or the fear of losing one's culture and traditions. Because the United States is such a mash-up of cultures, however, it's unclear what Americans fear losing. In fact, many Americans have no connection at all to the faraway lands their immigrant ancestors left to chase the American dream. They can't speak their ancestors' language and know little about their customs.

On the other hand, political scientists and economists say that people who fear immigrants worry that the newcomers will take their jobs or use up their resources. Yet, supporters of immigrants have repeatedly pointed out that newcomers to the United States often work in fields that lack enough American workers or that Americans simply don't want to enter, such as farm work.

Some Americans fear that if too many immigrants come to the United States, they will give birth to lots of children and change the face of what has historically been a white-majority nation. By 2050, racial minorities, or people of color, will make up 54 percent of the American population. At this point, whites will be in the minority, making up just 46 percent of the nation.[1] Today four states—Hawaii, California, Texas, and New Mexico—have more people of color than whites. The District of Columbia is also a majority-minority area. So far, these regions have managed to thrive.

FUTURE SCIENCE FROM THE CHILDREN OF IMMIGRANTS

The Intel Science Talent Search is one of the most important science competitions an American high school student can enter. Children of immigrants have excelled in the contest. In 2016, 83 percent of competition finalists were children of immigrants. Also, 75 percent of the children's parents were working in the country on H-1B visas. The government awards these travel papers to highly qualified immigrant workers. If the government stops skilled foreign workers from coming to the United States, their contributions will be missed, as will those of their children. Among the forty Intel finalists:

- Fourteen had both parents born in India.
- Eleven had both parents born in China.
- Seven had both parents born in the United States.
- Other finalists had parents born in Canada, Cyprus, Iran, Japan, Nigeria, Singapore, South Korea, and Taiwan.[4]

Throughout the country, immigrants of color might be a benefit, because the majority-white US population is aging, and immigrants tend to be young. Many European countries, as well as Japan, South Korea, and China, have a rapidly growing population of elders who will drive up health care costs. But the United States will likely avoid the problems related to an aging population.

FROM UNDOCUMENTED IMMIGRANT TO BRAIN SURGEON

Dr. Alfredo Quiñones-Hinojosa came from Mexico to the United States the day before he turned nineteen. With just $65, he crossed the border without the legal papers needed to enter the country. Almost penniless and unable to speak English, he picked vegetables and lived in a trailer, hoping the police wouldn't catch him. Later, he loaded fish and sulfur onto railroad cars and began taking night classes at San Joaquin Delta Community College.

Thanks to a program created by the 1986 Immigration Reform and Control Act, he got permission to work in the US and then a temporary green card. The speech and debate coach at the community college mentored Quiñones-Hinojosa and helped him apply to the University of California, Berkeley.

He began his studies at Berkeley in 1991, the same year he received permanent US residency. He earned a medical degree from Harvard Medical School and became a citizen in 1997. Today, he is a well-known doctor at Johns Hopkins University. There, he is a professor of neurosurgery and oncology as well as the director of the Brain Stem Tumor Cell Laboratory. He performs about 250 brain surgeries a year on patients and continues to perform research.

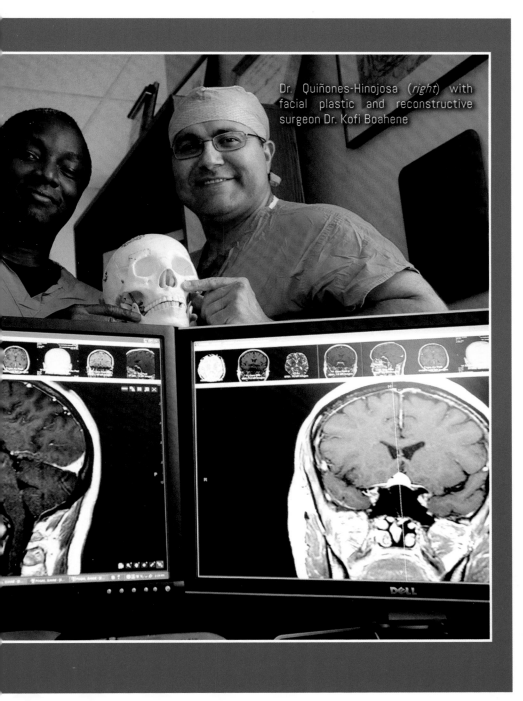

Dr. Quiñones-Hinojosa (*right*) with facial plastic and reconstructive surgeon Dr. Kofi Boahene

By 2050, about a third of Germans and Italians will be over the age of sixty-five. The average age of Germans will be fifty-one, while the average age of Americans will be forty-one.[2] Immigrants are increasing the number of children in America, which means that population growth is at about 28 percent. In countries such as Germany, China, and Japan, population growth has dropped. These countries will have trouble funding social welfare programs because they will have fewer young people in the workforce. This will not be the case in the United States.

So, while some Americans believe they have good reason to dislike immigrants, the data shows that immigration has given the country a boost. Immigration has not only helped the nation grow—it has also helped it become the most powerful country on the planet. The success of the United States is largely due to its history of welcoming many talented people from all over the globe. The country makes good use of their skills. In turn, immigrants return the favor. Immigrants have made an impact on many aspects of American life, particularly in the fields of science and technology.

IMMIGRANTS AND THE NOBEL PRIZE

The number of Nobel Prizes that immigrants have won on behalf of the United States shows how much these newcomers have given back to the country. More than one hundred foreign-born Nobel Prize winners have been honored for their work in the United States. A study by the National Foundation for American Policy found that since 2000, immigrants have won 40 percent of American Nobel Prizes in chemistry, medicine, and physics. Open immigration policies have led to the United States winning these prizes, and the country has become a destination for foreign researchers in science and technology, according to the NFAP.[3]

Venezuelan-born Baruj Benacerraf (*left*) won the Nobel Prize in Medicine in 1980 for his work in immunology.

IMMIGRANT STRIDES IN CANCER RESEARCH

Immigrants are leaving their mark on cancer research in the United States:

- According to Stuart Anderson, 42 percent of the 1,500 researchers at the nation's top seven cancer research centers are foreign born. This is a large number, since only 13 percent of the general US population is foreign born.
- At the University of Texas MD Anderson Cancer Center in Houston, Texas, 62 percent of researchers are immigrants. At Memorial Sloan-Kettering Cancer Center in New York City, 56 percent of researchers are.
- About 21 percent of these scientists were born in China, another 10 percent in India, and others came from Taiwan and South Korea. Before 1965, the US government banned immigrants from these countries from entering.[5]

Dr. Rainer Storb, head of Seattle's Transplantation Biology Program, has made important contributions in cancer research. Storb came to the United States on a Fullbright Fellowship in the 1960s. The researcher then became a citizen. He went on to launch the transplant program and helped start the Fred Hutchinson Cancer Research Center. Storb is the second most-quoted researcher in the field of oncology, the study of cancer.

Venezuela-born Baruj Benacerraf arrived to the United States in 1939. Ten medical schools rejected him because he was Jewish, but the University of Virginia offered him a spot. He became a US citizen and served as a doctor in the US Army. He then headed the Sidney Farber Institute, now the Dana-Farber Cancer Institute. In 1980, he won the Nobel Prize in Physiology or Medicine for his work on how the human body tells the difference between its own cells and intruders.[6]

More than two-thirds of full-time graduate students in physics and chemistry hail from abroad. They're not just contributing to the sciences, they're shaping the future of these fields.

LOOKING TOWARD THE FUTURE

As concerns about terrorism rise, the United States has come to view immigration differently. Terrorism is now an international problem. The United States began its War on Terror after the September 11, 2001, attacks on the World Trade Center and the Pentagon. But terrorist attacks, and efforts to stop them, have led to civilian deaths around the world. Americans are understandably afraid of extremists who kill innocent people. But as scary as extremists are, terrorist attacks in the United States remain rare. Also, when they do occur,

US citizens or permanent residents (82 percent) are more often to blame than immigrants or refugees (18 percent).[7] Thus, while the country must fight against terrorism, it seems clear that restricting immigration won't stop it.

Keeping immigrant scientists and researchers out of the United States will lead to serious problems for research institutions. Currently, 71 percent of full-time graduate students in electrical engineering, 65 percent of grad students in computer science, and 61 percent of grad students in industrial engineering are international students. Roughly 44 percent of full-time graduate students in physics and 40 percent in chemistry also come from overseas.[8]

Immigrants are the key to making America great and keeping it that way. If government policy in a changing political climate leaves them out, both they and the United States will suffer a great loss.

CHAPTER NOTES

CHAPTER 1

1. Woody Guthrie, "This Land Is Your Land," 1997, *This Land Is Your Land: The Asch Recordings, Vol. 1,* Smithsonian Folkways, audio CD.

CHAPTER 2

1. Curt Suplee, "Joseph Priestley: Discoverer of Oxygen," ACS. org, 2004, https://www.acs.org/content/dam/acsorg/education /whatischemistry/landmarks/josephpriestleyoxygen/joseph -priestley-discoverer-of-oxygen-commemorative-booklet.pdf.

CHAPTER 3

1. Ken Gewertz, "Albert Einstein, Civil Rights Activist," *Harvard Gazette,* April 12, 2007, http://news.harvard.edu/gazette /story/2007/04/albert-einstein-civil-rights-activist.

CHAPTER 4

1. "Elias A. Zerhouni, M.D.: Director, National Institutes of Health, May 2, 2002 - October 31, 2008," *The NIH Almanac,* October 22, 2015, https://www.nih.gov/about-nih/what-we-do/nih -almanac/elias-zerhouni-md.

2. "Budget," NIH.gov, March 6, 2017, https://www.nih.gov/about-nih /what-we-do/budget.

CHAPTER 5

1. "Elizabeth H. Blackburn – Biographical," Nobelprize.org, https://www.nobelprize.org/nobel_prizes/medicine/laureates/2009/blackburn-bio.html.

2. 2009, Ejeta. Dr. Gebisa Ejeta, Ethiopia," Worldfoodprize.org, https://www.worldfoodprize.org/en/laureates/20002009_laureates/2009_ejeta.

3. "All About Sorghum," Sorghumcheckoff.com, http://www.sorghumcheckoff.com/all-about-sorghum.

4. "Sorghum Production Guideline," nda.agric.za, March 2010, http://www.nda.agric.za/docs/Brochures/prodGuideSorghum.pdf.

5. Ibid.

6. Lisa Mastny, "Africa's Indigenous Crops," worldwatch.org, 2011, http://www.worldwatch.org/system/files/NtP-Africa%27s-Indigenous-Crops.pdf.

CHAPTER 6

1. David Warmflash, "Franklin Chang-Díaz: Propulsion Pioneer for Future Generations of Astronauts," Visionlearning.com, 2015, http://www.visionlearning.com/en/library/Inside-Science/58/Franklin-Chang-D%C3%ADaz/219.

2. "Franklin R. Chang-Díaz (Ph.D), NASA Astronaut (Former)," NASA.gov, September 2012, https://www.jsc.nasa.gov/Bios/htmlbios/chang.html.

3. Ibid.

4. "Kalpana Chawla – The Woman Who Loved to Fly: All About India's First Woman Astronaut," *The Indian Express*, March 17, 2017, http://

indianexpress.com/article/india/kalpana-chawala-woman-who
-loved-to-fly-all-about-indias-first-woman-astronaut-4572626.

5. "Kalpana Chawla (PhD), NASA Astronaut (Deceased)," NASA.gov,
May 2004, https://www.jsc.nasa.gov/Bios/htmlbios/chawla.html.

CHAPTER 7

1. Ashley Broughton, "Minorities Expected to Be Majority in 2050,"
CNN.com, August 13, 2008, http://www.cnn.com/2008/US/08/13
/census.minorities.

2. Olga Khazan, "Immigration Is the Only Reason the U.S. Doesn't
Have an Aging Crisis," *The Atlantic*, January 30, 2014, https://www
.theatlantic.com/health/archive/2014/01/immigration-is-the
-only-reason-the-us-doesnt-have-an-aging-crisis/283474.

3. "Immigrants and Nobel Prizes," NFAP.com, October 2016, http://
nfap.com/wp-content/uploads/2016/10/Immigrants-and-Nobel
-Prizes.NFAP-Policy-Brief.October-2016.pdf.

4. Stuart Anderson, "The Contributions of the Children of Immigrants
to Science in America," NFAP.com, March 2017, http://nfap
.com/wp-content/uploads/2017/03/Children-of-Immigrants-in-
Science.NFAP-Policy-Brief.March-2017.pdf.

5. Stuart Anderson, "Immigrant Scientists Invaluable to the United
States," NAFSA.org, May/June 2015, https://www.nafsa.org
/_/File/_/ie_mayjun15_front_lines.pdf.

6. Ibid.

7. Uri Friedman, "Where America's Terrorists Actually Come
From," *The Atlantic*, January 30, 2017, https://www.theatlantic
.com/international/archive/2017/01/trump-immigration-ban
-terrorism/514361.

8. Stuart Anderson, "The Increasing Importance of Immigrants to Science and Engineering in America," NFAP.com, June 2014, http://nfap.com/wp-content/uploads/2014/06/NFAP-Policy -Brief.Increasing-Importance-of-Immigrants-in-Science-and -Engineering.June-2014.pdf.

GLOSSARY

anthropology The study of human beings, especially their behavior, cultural artifacts, and how they form their societies.

asylum A safe haven for immigrants fleeing war, abuse, or other dangers in their home countries.

carbohydrate A particle made of hydrogen, carbon, and oxygen. They may contain sugars, starches, or cellulose.

cereal An edible grain or the plants that create it. Examples include wheat, corn, rye, sorghum, and oats.

ethnicity A way to describe a group of people who share language, culture, religion, or national origin.

fascism A type of government that demands strict respect for authority and punishes people who disagree or don't show national pride.

fission To divide or split into two parts; nuclear fission splits certain types of atoms and releases large amounts of energy.

fusion Combining two or more parts into one; nuclear fusion combines atoms to release large amounts of energy.

glycogen A type of carbohydrate that is the main storage form of glucose in cells.

hybrid plant A plant made by crossing two different kinds of plants to get improved results.

insulin A hormone made in the pancreas that balances blood sugar levels.

neutrino Tiny particles made when radioactive atoms decay.

neutron Tiny particle in the nucleus of an atom that is slightly bigger than a proton.

photosynthesis A process in which plants use sunlight to create food out of carbon dioxide and water and release oxygen as a by-product.

plasma One of the four states of matter, along with solid, liquid, and gas. It can help speed up rockets and carry them farther.

quantum mechanics A field of physics that explores how matter acts on the smallest scale.

refugee A person forced out of one's home country by war, persecution, or natural disaster.

space shuttle A spacecraft that can be used more than once to bring people and objects to space and back.

spacetime A physics concept in which time and space become one continuum, so space doesn't exist without time or vice versa.

telomere Repeating parts of DNA at the ends of chromosomes that protect the DNA strand.

transformer A device used to increase or lower the voltage of an alternating current of electricity.

voltage The amount of likely energy between two points on an electrical circuit.

xenophobia Fear or hatred of foreigners or people from a country other than one's own.

FURTHER READING

Anderson, Jennifer Joline. *Albert Einstein: Revolutionary Physicist.* Minneapolis, MN: Abdo Publishing, 2015.

Blackburn, Elizabeth and Elissa Epel. *The Telomere Effect: A Revolutionary Approach to Living Younger, Healthier, Longer.* New York: Grand Central Publishing, 2017.

Cooper, Christopher. *The Truth about Tesla: The Myth of the Lone Genius in the History of Innovation.* New York: Race Point Publishing, 2015.

Cunningham, Ann. *Critical Perspectives on Immigrants and Refugees.* New York: Enslow Publishing, 2016.

Etingoff, Kim. *Women in Chemistry. Major Women in Science.* Broomall, PA: Mason Crest, 2014.

Farish, Terry. *The Good Braider.* Los Vegas, NV: Amazon Children's Publishing, 2012.

Gibson, Karen Bush. *Women in Space: 23 Stories of First Flights, Scientific Missions, and Gravity-Breaking Adventures.* Chicago, IL: Chicago Review Press, 2014.

Goldenstern, Joyce. *Albert Einstein: Genius of the Theory of Relativity.* New York: Enslow Publishing, 2015.

Gonzales, Doreen. *The Secret of the Manhattan Project.* New York: Enslow Publishing, 2012.

Grimm, Joe. 100 *Questions and Answers about Arab Americans.* Michigan University School of Journalism Series on Cultural Competence. Canton, MI: Read the Spirit Books, 2014.

Quiñones-Hinojosa, Alfredo. *Becoming Dr. Q: My Journey from Migrant Farm Worker to Brain Surgeon.* Berkeley and Los Angeles: University of California Press, 2012.

Rusch, Elizabeth and Oliver Dominguez (Illustrator). *Electrical Wizard: How Nikola Tesla Lit Up the World*. Somerville, MA: Candlewick Press, 2015.

WEBSITES

Association of International Educators

www.nafsa.org/

The mission of the Association of International Educators is international education and exchange. The organization promotes understanding among people of various backgrounds. The organization advocates for an engaged and welcoming United States.

The Berkeley Nuclear Research Center

bnrc.berkeley.edu/Famous-Women-in-Physical-Sciences-and-Engineering

The Berkeley Nuclear Research Center has a special section on famous women in the sciences and engineering. BNRC addresses sustainability issues in the development of nuclear power. The website has a news tab that reports on all things nuclear.

The Encyclopedia of World Biography

www.notablebiographies.com

The Encyclopedia of World Biography, sponsored by Gale Publishing, provides a full listing of notable persons.

The National Science Foundation

www.nsf.gov/

The National Science Foundation is a federal agency that promotes science and research. NSF funds about a quarter of all federally supported basic research that America's colleges and universities do. The website provides, among other information, a document library.

Nobel Prize
www.nobelprize.org/nobel_prizes/lists/all/
The Nobel Prize website lists all the people who have won prizes in their various categories, including the sciences. The website also lists biographies, photographs, Nobel Prize speeches, interviews, and detailed descriptions of the work that won the awardees the honor.

The Statue of Liberty-Ellis Island Foundation
www.libertyellisfoundation.org/
The Statue of Liberty-Ellis Island Foundation includes historical landmarks and an immigration museum. It's also home to the American Family Immigration History Center, which makes more than 51 million Port of New York arrival records in the Ellis Island Archives available online. The website provides a history of immigrants who came through Ellis Island.

INDEX

ABOUT THE AUTHOR

MARYELLEN LO BOSCO

Maryellen Lo Bosco writes about literature, history, philosophy, and the life sciences. She has taught English language arts in high school and expository writing in college. She also has many years of experience as an academic editor in the social sciences. In the past decade, she has worked with writers of scholarly books in the field of psychoanalysis. She writes literature guides for both students and teachers and nonfiction books for teens. She tutors and teaches students in writing at Suffolk County Community College in Brentwood, New York.